# GODLY LEADERSHIP

## GROUP BIBLE STUDY

WRITTEN BY Jerry Hickson

*Godly Leadership: Group Bible Study*
Written by Jerry Hickson
© 2020 Warner Press Inc.

All rights reserved. No part of this publication may be reproduced, stored in a retrieval system, or transmitted in any form or by any means—electronic, mechanical, photocopy, recording, or any other method of storage—except for brief quotations in printed reviews, without the prior permission of the publisher.

Requests for information should be sent to:
Warner Press Inc.
P.O. Box 2499
Anderson, IN 46018
www.warnerpress.org

Unless otherwise noted, all Scripture references are from the Holy Bible, New International Version®, NIV® Copyright © 1973, 1978, 1984, 2011 by Biblica, Inc.® All rights reserved worldwide.

Kevin Stiffler • Editor
S. Katie Miller • Layout & Design

# CONTENTS



**The Warner Press *Relevance* Group Bible Studies** provide intriguing examinations of topics using the whole of the Scriptures. The guides incorporate various stories and activities to introduce and apply the subject matter, with a Bible study component at the heart of each session. Our goal is to show life-long believers and those new to the faith how to know the Lord intimately while encouraging them to step out and join him in his work with miraculous results.

These flexible studies are ideal for any setting. We know that time is a valuable commodity in today's society, and that's why each book consists of five or six short lessons intended to meet the group's scheduling needs.

# David Becomes King

2 Samuel 5:1–7; 6:1–5, 11–15, 17–18

## Main Point

At the proper time, David took the reigns as the king of Israel; effective leaders must establish their credibility with accomplishment.

## Background

Today's study includes the ascent of David to Israel's throne, the conquest of Jerusalem, and the move of the ark to Jerusalem. David was considered to be the greatest of all the kings of Israel. For years, much of the Promised Land had remained outside the control of the people of God. The ark of the covenant represented the presence of God among his people. Prior to David's rule the ark had been captured by the Philistines. While the ark was back in Israel, it had not been returned to its rightful place. As David took the throne, he restored the ark to its proper home in the capital city.

Who would you list as some of the most notable business, political, and religious leaders? What distinguishes these individuals as leaders?

What people have you known who have shown themselves to be exceptional leaders but never became famous or more widely known?

What is a situation in which you have been a leader or in which you may be required to lead in the near future?

What are some of the most the vexing problems of our time? in your community? in your country? in the world? in Christianity? in your church? How do these problems call for gifted leadership?

I. **Read** 2 Samuel 5:1–7.

What is significant about the statement, "We are your own flesh and blood" (v 1)? Was this expressing a qualification of David or the availability of the people? Explain.

Look at 1 Samuel 17:26, 48–51; 23:5; 30:1–6, 16–19 and 2 Samuel 1:17–18; 3:1. How had David proven himself previously as a leader?

Much of Canaan (the Promised Land) had remained in control of other nations, particularly cities and plains. Jerusalem had a central location on high ground. Why was the conquest of Jerusalem a significant achievement for David as a leader? Why was it important for David to establish a new center of government there?

What was a significant challenge you faced upon taking a new posit on of leadership? How did you respond? What was the outcome? What (if anything) would you do differently next time and why?

## II. Read 2 Samuel 6:1–5.

What do you imagine this parade looked like? What numbers of people were involved? What led the procession? What kinds of instruments are mentioned?

What kind of installation celebration was a part of your beginning in a new position? Describe the occasion. Was there an element of that celebration that involved God? How was God involved in your role as a leader—whether or not God was specifically acknowledged at the start?

_______________________________________________

_______________________________________________

_______________________________________________

_______________________________________________

## III. Read 2 Samuel 6:11–15.

Why was the ark of the covenant being moved a second time? Check out 6:6–10 for a clue.

_______________________________________________

_______________________________________________

_______________________________________________

What is the significance of the observation about the household of Obed-Edom the Gittite being blessed?

_______________________________________________

_______________________________________________

_______________________________________________

_______________________________________________

Why was the transfer of the ark such a cause for celebration? What does this imply about the reign of David as opposed to that of the previous administration?

When have you seen a group or organization blessed because of the presence of God there and the presence of godly people there?

## IV. Read 2 Samuel 6:17–18.

Why do you think the ark was moved to a new tent in Jerusalem instead of the old tabernacle in Shiloh? Joshua 18:1 and 1 Samuel 3:21 provide some context. What do you imagine happened to Shiloh and the tabernacle following the loss of the ark to the Philistines? See 1 Samuel 4.

How is it significant that David was fashioning a new tent as opposed to rebuilding the old tabernacle as instructed in Exodus 26?

To what degree is keeping God central important in a leadership role you play? Why?

## Qualifications for Leadership

Most job descriptions include requirements to qualify for the position, including education and experience. Whether it is a hired position or a volunteer opportunity, leadership requires certain characteristics and behaviors. Some qualifications are unique to the particular position, while others apply more universally to most leadership positions. Some of the qualifications for leadership are as much about character as they are about training or experience.

David proved himself worthy to be king through years of leadership during times when his authority was not recognized and his life was often threatened. When circumstances opened the door, David was enthusiastically followed by masses of people because he had clearly proven himself to be the right man for the job.

What would you say are the universal qualifications for leadership? Which of these qualifications are about character as opposed to skills?

What can you do right now to prove yourself that might make a difference
in future leadership opportunities?

## Devotion to God

It can probably be said that righteousness and devotion to God are beneficial for any leadership position. Leadership in the kingdom of God certainly demands a person who knows God and faithfully heeds the voice of God. David stepped into a void where the previous king had proven himself unwilling or incapable of following God faithfully. One consequence was that much of the land God had ordained as the Promised Land remained in foreign hands. Another consequence was that the ark—the symbol of God's presence—had been removed from its rightful place in God's house (the tabernacle at Shiloh). As "a man after [God's] own heart" (Acts 13:22), David saw the need to complete the conquest of the land given by God and to move the ark of the covenant from its temporary lodging to its rightful place as a testimony to the covenant between God and the people.

How does a leader today demonstrate devotion to God and fidelity to God's leading?

What are concrete actions that need to be taken in your organization, church, or community to reflect devotion to God?

## Completing Unfinished Business

A wise leader builds credibility by accomplishing achievable goals. A new leader has a limited ability to effect change; his or her work should focus initially on obvious problems that can be solved easily. With success will come greater ability to tackle more difficult or controversial issues. As Jesus said, "Whoever can be trusted with very little can also be trusted with much" (Luke 16:10).

For David, some of his earliest agenda included conquering the city of Jerusalem and moving the ark from its previous lodging. By establishing his capital at Jerusalem—which became known as the City of David—David was able to better govern all of Israel. By keeping the ark of the covenant in Jerusalem, David cemented his place as God's chosen leader for God's people. An effective leader wisely chooses priority issues to bring needed change and prove leadership credibility.

**What are examples of accomplishments by current leaders that establish their credibility?**

**How does failure to complete unfinished business hinder or even destroy a leader?**

What are some examples of issues that you need to address to be a better leader?

<br>
<br>
<br>
<br>
<br>

## Closing Prayer

Lord, everyone here is a leader, whether in a paid position or a volunteer role. We ask your blessing on us as leaders gathered here and on those we are called to influence. We pray for sensitivity to your leading in the decisions we make in the days to come. Give us insight on where we most need to focus our attention. Like David, may each of us prove to be the right leader for the right time. Amen. ∎

**L 2**

# King Solomon Seeks Wisdom

1 Kings 3:4–15; 4:29–30

## Main Point

Solomon sought a most important resource for leadership; discernment (or wisdom) is an essential requirement for those who lead.

## Background

Solomon was the son of David ordained to succeed the throne, and he had some pretty big shoes to fill. Since moving from slavery in Egypt to occupy the Promised Land, God's people had spent forty years in the desert under the leadership of Moses, about 400 years taking Canaan under the leadership of Joshua and the judges, and time under the kingships of Saul and David. This federation of twelve related family bands would not be easy to govern. Threats would be continually present from without and within. Solomon recognized that, beyond material resources and military might, he would require discernment in order to be an effective leader.

## Discernment

The selection of a new leader is usually a time of excitement, at least for that particular leader and those who are supportive of this choice. Often a new leader is faced with one or several crises that must be immediately addressed. Most do their best to work with those to whom they are accountable and are particularly glad for those who offer support, but decisions must be made. Leaders simply must be capable of making sound judgments. Any venture is bound to present some "do or die" issues where making the right decision has significant consequences. This is true in politics, in the military, in business, in ministry, and pretty much anywhere.

**Besides discernment or wisdom, what other qualities can you think of that are essential or important for leadership?**

**What examples can you list of leaders who have demonstrated glaringly poor discernment? How about leaders who model excellent wisdom?**

What is an issue where you have had to make a decision that required sub-
stantial wisdom or discernment?

Solomon was not the obvious choice for leadership. His father had started as a mere shepherd. His mother was the infamous Bathsheba, whose first child with David had not survived. David had older sons, at least one of whom had eyes on the throne and had recently continued to conspire against Solomon (1 Kings 1—2). Why do you think God chose Solomon for this role?

Why was Solomon going to Gibeon to offer sacrifices? Why not Shiloh or Jerusalem? See Joshua 18:1; 1 Samuel 3:21; 2 Samuel 6:17–18; and Jeremiah 7:12 for some context. What was a "high place" (v 4)? What did this event imply as the new king was beginning his reign?

What do you make of Solomon's declaration that he was "only a little child" (v 7)? Was this about chronological age or something else? Explain. What did this imply about Solomon's heart?

In what ways do you feel like "only a child" when you consider the responsibilities that lie before you?

From verse 11, what alternatives could Solomon have chosen for himself rather than asking for a discerning heart? Why might these other things have been expected of and even beneficial to a nation's leader? What did Solomon's request for wisdom imply about his priorities?

God made some stellar promises to Solomon. What were the conditions that accompanied these promises (v 14)? What was implied if these conditions were to be broken?

Why do you think the Lord chose to speak to Solomon in a dream? What did Solomon do after the dream? Do you think this was a response to the content of the dream or just the completion of what he had come to Gibeon to do? Explain.

As you take on a new assignment, what do you see as the qualities or personal resources you most need? Why?

## II. Read 1 Kings 4:29–30.

What other indications do you know of that Solomon's prayer for wisdom was granted? See 1 Kings 3:16–28, 1 Kings 10:1–13, and much of the Book of Proverbs for some examples.

Solomon was well-known for his wisdom, but what other less-positive things also became a part of his reputation?

Who is one of the wisest leaders you have ever worked with? How did this person demonstrate exceptional discernment?

<br><br>

When your life is over, what do you hope people will say about the mark you left behind and the kind of leader you were?

## Restructuring

In the late 1990s, the North American offices of the Church of God (based in Anderson, Indiana) found it necessary to dramatically restructure their organization. In recent years the Church of God has again been faced with challenges requiring restructuring at the highest levels. A key component was and is choosing an individual with the wisdom required to overcome resistance to change and mobilize resources to more effectively reach the world today and tomorrow.

In any venture, leadership requires wisdom. The leader must interface effectively with others and must take appropriate risks. Solomon was noted for his wisdom, whether in the story of the women in conflict over a baby or in the collection of much of the Hebrew wisdom literature. Among Solomon's achievements was the building of the great temple in Jerusalem. Just holding the kingdom together in the wake of his father's reign was evidence of Solomon's greatness, as revealed by the division of the nation that happened soon after Solomon died.

What are some of the challenges leaders today face that require wisdom or discernment?

What current challenges do you face that require wisdom or discernment in your own leadership?

**Solomon's Prayer**

The word used in the original biblical language of Hebrew for *wisdom* implies hearing well and obeying the voice of God. When we understand that God's authority includes everything in life, we recognize that respect for God's commands is foundational to all decision making. Many in the world of business today are recognizing the need for ethics in leadership. Leaders must be people of integrity who model and reproduce among their co-workers the ability to know right from wrong and to act responsibly. Failure to act with wisdom or discernment often results in scandal and economic disaster. We should all pray for godly wisdom in our leaders.

**What does godly wisdom or discernment look like?**

**How do godly leaders effectively transmit their integrity and discernment to those who serve under them?**

What are you doing (or can you do) to better hear the voice of God and understand the implications for your own leadership?

## Faithful amidst Diversity

One challenge for godly leadership today is the mosaic of religious views found in society. Some call ours a "post-Christian" culture. Respect for diversity is demanded, including accepting those whose moral values differ from biblical norms. Is this really all that different from the world faced by Solomon? Clearly, he was in a context that was polytheistic. Solomon himself failed at times to refrain from conforming to practices that were not faithful to God. The prophetic voice found in the Bible rarely if ever counsels tolerance in the face of conflict with God's express commands. One response by some today is to disregard the teaching of God's Word as narrow-minded or bigoted.

**Where do you find challenges to obeying biblical teaching as non-practical or offensive?**

How can we act with wisdom and discernment when the values of those around us conflict with our understanding of the Bible or God's expectations?

## Closing Prayer

Lord, we pray for wisdom in the decisions that each of us have to make in our workplaces and the other places where we are given opportunities to influence others. May we always have a keen ear for your leading. May the things we say and do prove to be appropriate and beneficial for others. Help us especially to have the wisdom to set the right course in the face of all the competing perspectives that surround us. Amen. ■

**L 3**

# Josiah Remembers the Covenant

2 Chronicles 34; 2 Kings 22 — 23

## Main Point

Josiah worked to lead the nation back to faithfulness to their covenant with God; good leadership includes fidelity to core values and mission.

## Background

Josiah became king at the age of eight. Ten years into his reign, a discovery was made while cleaning neglected rooms in the temple. God's people had lost God's Word. This was indicative of the apostasy of the Israelites for many generations. With the reading of God's Law (perhaps the Book of Deuteronomy) came repentance and a spirit of revival. Sadly, this new day was short-lived; King Josiah was killed in battle, and not long after that the Babylonians conquered Jerusalem and destroyed the temple. But the time of revival represented one of the high points in the history of the Old Testament, particularly of the kings following Solomon.

**Lee Iacocca and Chrysler**

Chrysler, which had long been one of the "big three" American auto-makers and was the tenth-largest corporation in the United States, was near collapse by the end of the 1970s. A government bailout of $1.5 billion was provided, and a new chairman stepped up. Lee Iacocca had previously been famous for his work at Ford, particularly related to the launch of the Mustang sports car. Central to the recovery of Chrysler was the K-car and the minivan. Within five years, the government-guaranteed loans were repaid and Chrysler was on track again as a member of the "big three."

What examples can you list of organizations and causes that have been sidetracked from their historic values and missions? How about churches you know of that have lost their focus?

What examples can you list of leaders who have led their organizations through a process of reform and revitalization?

What examples can you list of Christian leaders who have effectively brought revival to churches or Christian organizations or causes?

I. **Read** 2 Chronicles 34.

How effective could an eight-year-old really be in leading a nation? How about in doing what is right in God's eyes? Describe examples you know of children or teens who proved themselves to be strong or effective leaders.

How significant is it that Josiah was leading the nation in reform before the discovery of the lost Book of the Law? What were the components of the reform mentioned in this account?

Churches and other organizations sometimes bury time capsules or commission official historical records. In what significant ways was finding the Book of the Law different from discovering some long-lost element of history?

How could it be that the Scriptures had been lost for so long?

What was the result of reading from the newly discovered Book of the Law?

What examples can you think of where a company, church, or other organization you were involved with had to destroy idols that had distracted them from their mission?

What examples of return-to-first principles can you recall from your own story? Describe a time when you had to "get back to the Bible."

What would change if people would take the word of the Bible seriously?

## II. Read 2 Kings 22 – 23.

Why did Josiah tear his robes when the words of the Book of the Law were read to him? What somber conclusion did he come to? How did God confirm this conclusion? What does this have to teach us about our own response or lack of response to God's Word?

When have you participated in or witnessed a covenant renewal ceremony? Describe the situation. Why was this ceremony done? What effect was it intended to have? What effect did it actually have? Explain.

How could there have been so many vile religious practices among God's people?

What do you make of the statement made in 2 Kings 23:22? What examples can you think of where a company, church, or other organization had a particularly meaningful celebration that marked an important historical event?

What differences do you note between the account from 2 Chronicles 34 and that of 2 Kings 22—23? What do you notice about the chronological placement of Josiah's reforms in each story? What (if any) difference does this make?

What do you make of the way Josiah's life ended? Why do you think God didn't allow this good king to stick around longer? Why do you think Josiah's religious reforms seemed to just evaporate once he had passed from the scene?

## The Book of the Law

"The Book of the Law" found in the temple was obviously a lost document taking the people back to the covenant with God made under Moses. Many scholars believe it was the Book of Deuteronomy. Some of the things found there include:

- A summary of the conquest of the Promised Land (Deut 1—3)
- A prohibition of idolatry (Deut 4:1–40)
- A presentation of the Ten Commandments (Deut 5:5–21)
- The Shema, which would become the key expression of the Israelites' faith (Deut 6:4–5)
- A command to eradicate ungodly influences and remain faithful to the Lord (Deut 7—8)
- A reminder of the golden calf incident (Deut 9:7—10:11)
- A call to faithfulness (Deut 10:12—11:32)
- A comparison of godly worship with current practices (Deut 12—15)
- The command to observe the Passover and other holidays (Deut 16)
- Other details of the Law (Deut 17—26)
- A list of curses and blessings (Deut 27—28)
- A call to future generations to reform (Deut 29—30)
- A prediction of future rebellion (Deut 31:26–29)

In your own contexts (church, workplace, family, etc.), where might you be required to lead to a return to original mission and values? Explain.

**Elements of Renewal**

In his book *Dynamics of Spiritual Life: An Evangelical Theology of Renewal* (Downers Grove, IL: InterVaristy Press, 1979), Richard F. Lovelace provides a study of Christian revival. Based on his research of the great historic revivals of Christianity (including the First and Second Great Awakenings and the Jesus People Movement of the late 1960s and early 1970s), Lovelace suggests there are two things that must happen before revival can occur: an awareness of God and God's holiness and an awareness of our own sinful state. Primary emphases of any revival or spiritual renewal will include justification, sanctification, and the indwelling of the Holy Spirit. As participants apply the Scriptures to current issues, they will experience "disenculturation"—rethinking some old social rules and making new ones.

In your own opinion or experience, what are the key elements in revival or spiritual renewal?

What are the basic elements of revival or renewal that are required for you to be an effective leader in your particular settings?

## Destroying Idols

Today's passages mention several religious items that are not necessarily familiar to us today:

- Baal (pronounced BAY-ALL) was a male fertility god worshipped by the nations that predated Israel in the area.
- Asherah (or Ashtoreth) poles were erected to worship the female partner of Baal.
- Chemosh was the god of the neighboring Moabites known for the practice of infant sacrifice.
- Molek was the god of the neighboring Ammonites.

The term "high places" refers to multiple locations that were focal points for pagan worship and provided alternatives to worshipping the one true God at the temple in Jerusalem. These pagan centers were a problem for the people of God throughout their history. The northern and southern kingdoms were finally brought to an end as God had promised would happen if the people were not faithful to their original covenant.

Our own culture has its own religious practices that distract from biblical faith. In any enterprise, there are issues that distract us from pursuing the original mission of the organization.

**What are some of the idols that have arisen in our time?**

What are the idols that must be destroyed in order for *you* to be true to your values and mission?

## Closing Prayer

Lord, we confess that at times we have grown cold or lazy in our faith. In light of our study today, we ask that in everything we do we would be true to our core values and principles. We pray for repentant hearts that will make whatever changes are required. May our actions in the coming days result in a new season of effectiveness, not only in our own lives but in the lives of those we influence. Amen. ■

# Jesus Appoints Disciples

Mark 3:13–19; 6:6b–13, 30

## Main Point

Jesus selected a small group from the masses who followed him for special instruction to continue what he began; effective leadership requires training others to multiply the work.

## Background

Jesus had a large group of people following him, especially in the earlier days of his ministry. A smaller group of twelve people were chosen to spend significant time with the Master; they went on to become known as apostles of the faith. Three of the twelve men listed as Jesus' disciples (Peter, James, and John) were an inner circle. While Jesus was still with his disciples, he sent them on "trial runs" to practice what they had learned from him. Luke tells of sending the Twelve (Luke 9:1–9) but also such a mission involving seventy-two followers (Luke 10:1–24).

## To College or Not?

Training comes in different forms. Many choose to attend college for four years or more, leading to a baccalaureate degree. Some enroll in a community college for two years and then transfer to a four-year college. Some stop with an associate degree that qualifies them for the workforce. Some continue formal education to complete a master's degree or even a doctorate. There have always been some who do not choose the academic route to prepare for their life's work. Skilled trades use an apprenticeship process to prepare persons for certification as masters in their craft. Some have used stints in the military as their path for moving into adulthood. With the costs of formal academics skyrocketing, there are increasing proposals for a re-emphasis on alternative forms of training. Even traditional colleges are providing new formats, including night classes for adults and on-line degree programs.

What is a time when you were chosen to be part of a team or project? How was it that you were chosen? Was there an application process? Was there a training and/or internship process? Describe the situation.

When have you been the one to recruit others for a team or project? What went into your selection process, and why?

I. Read Mark 3:13–19.

Jesus spent around three years in his public ministry. One of the most important things he did (aside from his act on the cross) was to prepare the handful of people who would provide leadership for the church after he was gone. Through these few, Jesus would truly change the world. Is going up on a mountainside simply a statement of geography or a metaphor for something else? What do you think was involved in this process of Jesus deciding on the twelve men whom he would train and pour his life into?

For what purposes did Jesus call this select group of followers? What do you imagine went into the time that Jesus spent with the Twelve? What do you make of the two components Mark lists in the initial ministry experience Jesus commissioned for his disciples?

What do you notice in this list of names? Which of the names do you recognize from other accounts and which are unknown? What do you know about the various personalities mentioned? What do you make of the fact that we know so much about some of these men and so little about others?

Why do you think that all of the names listed here are male? From a cultural and practical standpoint, why would this have made sense? What other Bible passages (both Old and New Testament) indicate that God calls women to lead, prophesy, serve, and minister?

## II. Read Mark 6:6b–13.

What is significant about sending the disciples out two by two? How might we be wise to incorporate such an approach in ministry training and practice today?

What instructions did Jesus give the Twelve for their trial run? Why do you think he addressed these points? Why the emphasis on "packing light"? What is the meaning of "shaking the dust off one's feet"? What instructions might Jesus give if he were physically among us today? Why?

In what ways did the Twelve replicate the work of Jesus in their own ministries? How is this relevant for us today? How do we know when we're ready to "try it on our own"?

## III. Read Mark 6:30.

What is to be learned from this time of the Twelve reporting back to the Master after practicing the things he had called them to do? What is the benefit for the trainees? for the one doing the training? How would we be wise to incorporate similar report-back sessions in our ministry practices today?

## Recruiting Staff

Whether it is hiring workers or getting people to volunteer, a significant component in leadership is recruiting. Effective recruiting multiplies the output of the leader, while poor recruiting drains the energy of the leader and minimalizes results. Too often, we try to coax people into doing something they really don't want to do. Guilt is frequently used as a motivator. Understating the challenge that will be presented ("It's no big deal") is not an effective recruiting practice. Another common error is relying too much on published articles, posters, or announcements ("We'll take any warm body!") instead of directly approaching a person whom we believe is suited for the job. One of the key responsibilities of any leader is choosing the right people to help accomplish the mission.

What are some of your greatest successes in recruiting people? Is there a notable failure of recruiting that you can share?

What have you found to be the most effective ways to recruit workers?

## Training for Leadership

Once leaders have recruited a team, they must properly train their staff. John Maxwell and others have called attention to a basic process for equipping people for leadership:

1.   I do it while you watch.
2.   You do it while I watch.
3.   You do it and report back to me.
4.   You act on your own.

Even after initial training, leadership includes interacting with workers at an appropriate level. In *The One Minute Manager* (New York: William Morrow, 1982), Ken Blanchard says there are four styles of leadership: direction, coaching, support, and delegation. Subordinates tend to over-estimate the level of supervision they need, while supervisors tend to under-invest the correct amount of supervision. While leaders hope to recruit well-trained and experienced people, ongoing training continues to be required.

What is an example of "on-the-job training" that really made a difference for you? What was it that made this a good experience?

What have you found to be effective in training people to assist you in getting something done? Why?

## Reporting Back

Evaluation is an essential component of leadership, particularly when training others. Overlooking intentional evaluation is an easy error to make—to our detriment. Feedback and reports are tools we can use to evaluate the effectiveness of programs and people. When we study results and determine corrective action, it can help to harness or sustain the initial momentum of a new plan or objective. Sometimes evaluation is perceived to be uncomfortable or inconvenient, so it is neglected in favor of just "pushing ahead" with the work. Wisdom calls for allowing staff to participate in self-evaluation by "reporting back" what they have experienced. The leader should listen as much as criticize or make suggestions. Brainstorming can also be useful when practiced as a part of evaluation.

**Why are times of evaluation or reporting back so essential to training?**

**Where might you be wise to include intentional times or processes of feedback as part of training others?**

## Closing Prayer

Lord, we pray today not only for the leaders gathered here but also for those we are blessed to lead. We pray for the relationships we have with these people, and that we would model well the course that needs to be taken. Help us to listen and observe carefully and to guide and correct kindly. We pray for your leading and blessing as training opportunities and evaluations are established, that the results would truly change the world. Amen. ∎

# Choosing Special Workers

Acts 6; 7:1–2, 51–60

## Main Point

The apostles realized that we should make the best use of our specific gifts in God's work; effective leaders adopt priorities that call on all involved to give their best.

## Background

Today's passage includes a problem that recurred throughout the life of the first-century church. Dissension arose in Jerusalem among Christians of different ethnic backgrounds; in this case a dispute developed regarding the distribution of food to widows. Stephen was one of seven people chosen to help deal with the immediate problem, but his gifts also included wonders, signs, and godly wisdom. He testified that Jesus was "the Righteous One" (Acts 7:52)—the Messiah of Israel. Stephen did not hesitate to use his gifts for God's glory, even though it drew the criticism of others and eventually resulted in his death.

## Church Organization

Most church bylaws would probably be a good thing to read if you were having trouble falling asleep. They are a unique combination of policies and rules of order for a congregation to exist as a legal corporate entity in its state and also for the leadership, boards, and committees of the church to function. In the early church there were no bylaws, but steps were taken to provide formal leadership and address issues that arose.

Are you familiar with the bylaws of your local congregation or of another church you have been a part of? If so, what do they contain? What, if anything, is particularly wise or unique about them?

_______________________________________________

_______________________________________________

_______________________________________________

_______________________________________________

_______________________________________________

What qualifications should be necessary for someone to vote on the affairs of a congregation (pastoral leadership, lay leadership, purchasing property, etc.)?

_______________________________________________

_______________________________________________

_______________________________________________

_______________________________________________

What qualifications should be necessary for someone to serve in the leadership of a congregation?

What are some things that are not typically found in church bylaws but might be good to have there? Why?

I. **Read** Acts 6:1–7.

What was the problem that arose in the early church? When have you seen ethnic differences cause tension in the church or another group? How was the situation dealt with?

_______________________________________________

_______________________________________________

_______________________________________________

_______________________________________________

_______________________________________________

_______________________________________________

Would you consider Paul's description of the issue (v 2) derogatory, or do you think he meant something else by it? Explain.

_______________________________________________

_______________________________________________

_______________________________________________

_______________________________________________

What is different about the way the early church selected leaders here versus the way your own congregation selects leaders?

_______________________________________________

_______________________________________________

_______________________________________________

Verse 7 seems to indicate that the continued growth of the early church was enabled by the commitment and involvement of these seven laypersons to provide ministry leadership. How is this still true in the church today?

Is there a way that *every* member of the body of Christ can be involved in leadership and service? Is every person in the church even gifted for such a role? Explain. Take a look at 1 Corinthians 12:4–11 and Matthew 20:25–28 for some perspective on the use of our spiritual gifts in the church and the nature of leadership in God's kingdom.

## II. Read Acts 6:8 — 7:2.

What do "wonders and signs" have to do with distributing food to widows? What does this story have to teach us about the importance of the church's ministries and also the gifts needed by those who serve in those ministries?

What was it that made it impossible for Stephen's opponents to win an argument with him? What did they then resort to? How have you seen such an order of events play out in an organization (church or otherwise) today?

Stephen's answer to the charges against him stretches on for most of chapter 7. Why do you think he responded with more than a simple statement of denial?

## III. Read Acts 7:51–60.

What does it mean to be "stiff-necked" in this context? What other negative terms did Stephen use to describe the behavior of his opponents? Was he being rude or just being truthful? What kinds of trouble can being "stiff-necked" get people into—in the church and elsewhere?

What does the fact that Stephen could see the glory of God in heaven and Jesus standing at God's right hand indicate about God's opinion of Stephen's behavior? How might this vision have been helpful to Stephen at the time?

The Book of Acts is full of stories of the miraculous deliverance of God's people from danger. Why, in this case, do you think the Lord allowed Stephen to perish?

### Is It Worth It?

With just five minutes until worship started, Pastor Bridget scrambled to find someone to staff the church nursery for the morning. Several parents were waiting to drop off their little ones, but no volunteer had shown up—and the person in charge of recruiting those volunteers had not shown up and was not picking up her phone. It was the third time since June that this had happened. Pastor Bridget had to deliver the sermon; she could not stay in the nursery. She hated to pin nursery duty on one of the waiting parents at the last minute. And besides, nursery volunteers were required to undergo screening and background checks first. Bridget thought to herself, *Is it worth it? Is this ministry developing the type of servant-leaders we need?*

In the church, how do problems arise that are due to circumstances beyond our control? that are caused by the issues of individual Christians? that are by a combination of factors? How should godly and effective leaders respond?

Why is faith in Christ not an automatic "fix" for the troubles of life—at least not in the ways we often imagine?

## Effective Ministry



Today's story from Acts doesn't tell us how many widows relied on the church's food distribution program. Based on at least a few thousand believers (Acts 2:41) and a committee of seven, how big do you think this particular ministry was? Why?

Number of participants and giving or budget are common ways to evaluate the success of a church. What might be some more effective ways to gauge the success of a church or a particular ministry within the church? Explain.

## Effective Witness

The distribution of food to widows was not the only way God used Stephen to make a difference. Stephen performed signs and wonders due to God's grace and power in his life, and he effectively spoke in defense of the faith. It seems that no job was "beneath" him; he was willing to walk through whatever doors God opened in order to serve and witness in Jesus' name.

Service and witness go hand in hand. The life of Stephen demonstrated his willingness to do what might be considered a menial and ordinary job as a part of living out his faith. Sometimes our most effective witness is not in what we say but in what we do. The real power of an effective witness comes from giving our lives to help others.

How have you seen a practical ministry such as food distribution make a significant difference in witnessing to the love of God?

How have you personally participated in a practical ministry that made a significant difference in witnessing to the love of God?

**Closing Prayer**

Lord God, we thank you for the opportunity to use our creative abilities in service to others. We are grateful for the love and beauty of the body of Christ, the church. As we serve in your name, help us to do our best. Give us the courage to face difficult situations and hostile people who seem to scorn the gospel witness. Grant us the vision to see beyond today through your hope that burns eternal in our hearts. Amen. ∎

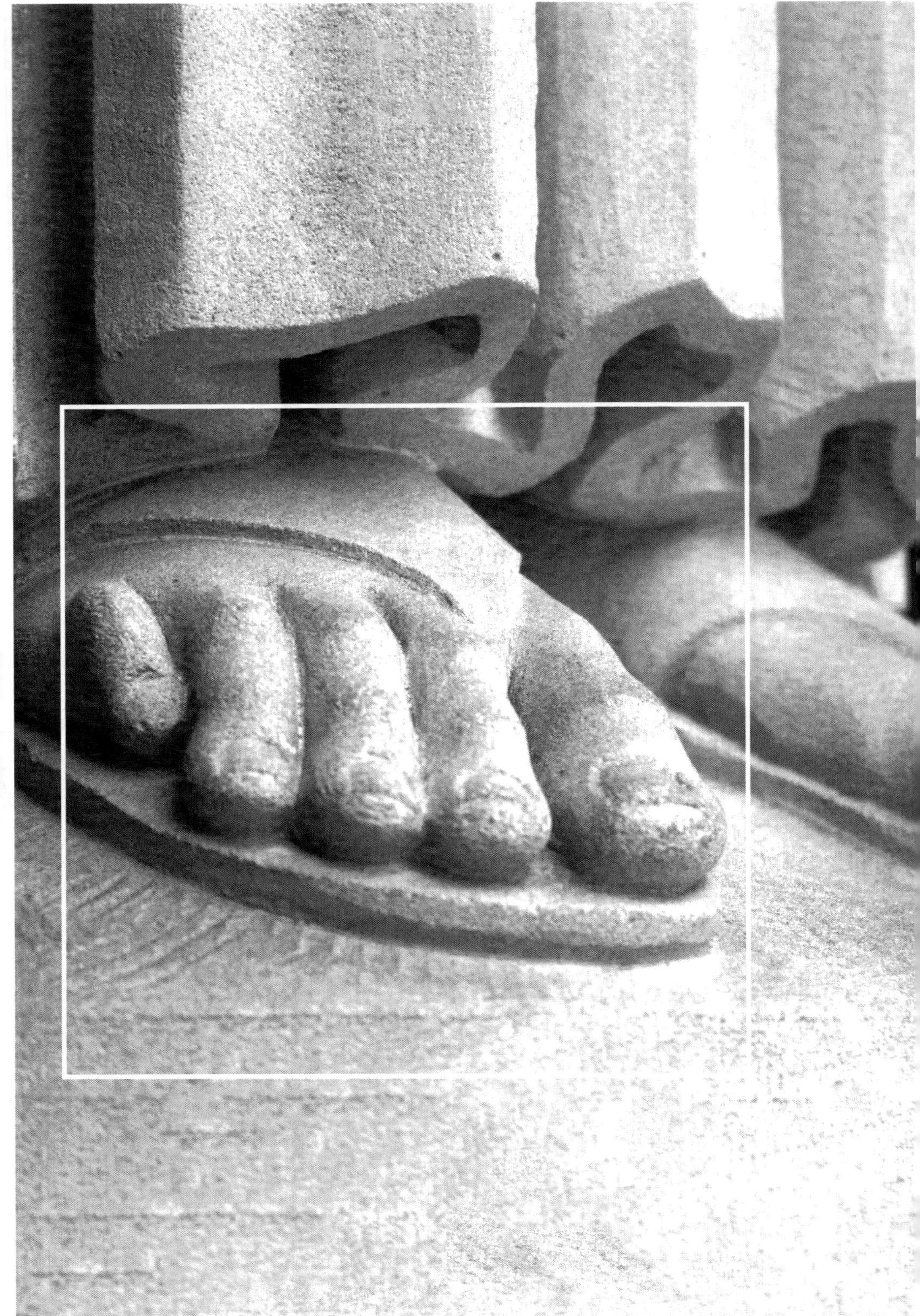

# Serving One Another

John 13:1–17

## *Main Point*

Jesus washed the feet of his closest followers; godly leadership is about servanthood and intimacy.

## *Background*

A key event on the night Jesus was betrayed leading to his crucifixion was when he washed the feet of his closest followers. This event s described only in the Gospel of John. It happened during the Passover, perhaps the greatest of the Jewish or Old Testament holidays. The other Gospels tell of the way Jesus transformed the Passover meal into Communion. But in John we have a very different event that speaks to the core of what leadership is. This event is the basis for the believers' practice of footwashing. While servanthood is an obvious theme, we should also notice the theme of intimacy or personal connection.

Where are you seeing the theme of servant leadership being advocated these days?

What is one of your fondest memories of a mentor who made a personal connection with you?

I. Read John 13:1–5.

Why is the timing mentioned in verse 1 so critical to this account? Where does this account fit in the narrative of Jesus' last days before his arrest, trial, and crucifixion?

What do you know about the Passover meal? Why is that relevant to this account? What is missing from this account of the Last Supper that is included in the other Gospels? Why do you think John chose to focus on th s part of the evening?

Why did John include the detail about the conspiracy by Judas Iscariot (v 2)? See also Matthew 26:14–16; Mark 14:10–11; and Luke 22:1–6. What do you think the behavior of this one of the Twelve did for the mindsets of the other eleven? What does this add to the meaning of this account?

Why did John include the comment about Jesus' mindset at the beginning of this account (v 3)? What contrast do you see between the attitude of Jesus and that of the disciples? What does this tension add to the dynamic of the story?

What is significant about the act of washing feet? Who usually took care of this chore? How do you think it felt for Jesus' followers to watch the Master wrap a towel around his waist and kneel at their feet? Why?

## II. Read John 13:6–11.

Why did Simon Peter object to having his feet washed? What do you think was going on inside Peter's head? How would you have reacted had you been one of those sitting around the table?

What did Jesus mean by saying "Unless I wash you, you have no part with me" (v 8)? Was he speaking only of the towel and basin or of some deeper issue? What is the lesson here? How might our own objections become obstructions to relationship with Jesus?




What do you make of Peter's statement in verse 9 and Jesus' statement in verse 10? What does this say about Peter's heart? What lesson can we learn from Jesus' response? Do you ever catch yourself going a little overboard in your desire to receive all that Christ has for you? How might Jesus be telling you to "chill out"?

## III. Read John 13:12–17.

When Jesus said that we should wash one another's feet, to what degree was he speaking symbolically as opposed to ordaining a religious observance? If you have experienced the ordinance of footwashing, describe it here.

_______________________________________________

_______________________________________________

_______________________________________________

_______________________________________________

What was Jesus saying in verse 16? How important is this issue for us? In what ways do you need to better emulate the example of Jesus?

_______________________________________________

_______________________________________________

_______________________________________________

_______________________________________________

## Training by Example

Jesus not only died for us. he also showed us how to live. If we take seriously the incarnation (that Jesus was fully human as well as fully divine), then we can and should replicate the life that Jesus lived as a model. On his last night with his disciples, Jesus said, "I have set you an example that you should do as I have done for you" (John 13:15). He further said, "Now that you know these things, you will be blessed if you do them" (John 13:17). While these words are rightly associated with the act of washing feet and of the servant heart demonstrated, we can extend this to an imperative to be imitators of all that Jesus modeled in his life.

How might we do well to put more emphasis on the life of Jesus?

How much of what you have learned has been by observation as much as instruction (caught as much as taught)? Have you seen times when what someone was trying to teach was contradicted by the life he or she was living? Explain.

## Servant Leadership

Ever since the publication of an essay by Robert K. Greenleaf in 1970, servant leadership has been seen in many quarters as essential. C. S. Lewis said, "The great thing, if one can, is to stop regarding all of the unpleasant things as interruptions of one's 'own,' or 'real' life. The truth is of course that what one calls the interruptions are precisely one's real life—the life God is sending one day by day: what one calls one's 'real life' is a phantom of one's own imagination" (*The Quotable Lewis* [Wheaton, IL: Tyndale House, 1989], 335). Jesus recognized as well as anyone that the road to leadership is service. Many Christian colleges are now using the gift of a towel as a symbol for sending graduating students off to their responsibilities of leadership.

**Why is servanthood such a vital component of leadership?**



**What examples can you list of people who have effectively demonstrated servant leadership?**



**In your own experience, how has servanthood proven to be necessary for effectively fulfilling a leadership role?**

## Intimacy in Leadership

We cannot really lead others without entering into relationship with them. As John Maxwell says, "You can love people without leading them, but you cannot lead people without loving them" (*Developing the Leader Within You* [Nashville: Thomas Nelson, 1993], 8). Footwashing is commonly seen as an act of servanthood, but it is also an act of deep intimacy. Feet are personal; not everyone washes my feet, and I do not wash just anyone's feet. The one who touches my feet is my brother or sister. For me to wash your feet is a statement of intimate relationship. If real leadership is to happen, the leader must bare his or her own soul and must connect with others on a personal level. This dynamic of intimacy is especially critical in leadership training.

**In what ways have you found it true that leadership is about making personal connections?**

**What do you recall in your own learning when someone used intimacy to prepare you for leadership?**

What can you do to establish more personal relationships with people who are leading or are being trained for leadership?

---

## Closing Prayer

Lord, we pray that as we carry out our leadership responsibilities, we would be effective in serving those entrusted to us. Make us willing to be vulnerable through intimacy as we serve, as Jesus taught and modeled for us. Give us eyes to see where we can best connect with others, so that by your Spirit you can change their lives according to your will and plan. Now that we know these things, bless us as we do them. Amen. ◾